Wallace & Gromit™ in A CLOSE SHAVE™

Student's Book

Peter Viney and Karen Viney

OXFORD

UNIVERSITY PRESS

Contents

Meet Wallace and Gromit™

Before you watch episode one

1 **Ask and answer these questions.**

Have you heard of Wallace and Gromit?

○ Yes, I have. ○ No, I haven't.

Have you seen Wallace and Gromit before?

○ Yes, I have. ○ No, I haven't.

If 'yes' …

Did you see them on television? / on video? / on DVD? / at the cinema?

I saw them …

Have you seen Wallace and Gromit in English?

○ Yes, I have. ○ No, I haven't.

Have you seen Wallace and Gromit in your own language?

○ Yes, I have. ○ No, I haven't.

Have you bought any Wallace and Gromit products?

○ Yes, I have. ○ No, I haven't.

If 'yes' …

What did you buy?

I bought …

2 **Have you seen … ? Ask your partner about a film, a TV programme and a song.**
e.g.

Have you seen ('Chicken Run')?

Have you seen ('Friends')?

Have you heard ('When I'm 64')?

3 **Change partners. Ask and answer questions about your first partner.**
e.g.

Has she seen ('Chicken Run')?

Has he heard ('When I'm 64')?

See: Grammar, page 12, Present perfect, Past simple

The uninvited guest

Watching the video

SECTION ONE 00.00 **TO** 01.27

> Teacher's note: Exploit section one first, then watch all of sections two, three and four before exploiting section by section.

Before you watch

1 Complete the spaces in this table.

Present	is	isn't			turn		open	
Past	was		drove	stopped		closed		heard

📺 Watch section one.

After you watch

2 Complete the sentences.

1 It _____ two o'clock in the morning but Gromit _____ asleep.

2 He _____ a noise.

3 It _____ a lorry. It _____ at the traffic-lights.

4 Gromit _____ a sheep.

5 Then he _____ footsteps.

6 A door _____.

7 And _____ again.

8 The traffic-lights _____ green.

9 And the lorry _____ away.

See: Grammar, page 12

4

SECTIONS 2,3,4

SECTION TWO   01.28 TO 02.50

Before you watch

1 Find five mistakes in the sign.

WALLACE 'N' GROMIT'S

WASH & GO

DOOR CLEANING SERVICE

Phone 1234

 Watch all of episode one.

After you watch

2 Make sentences about the pictures. Use the words from the box.

e.g. *Something has eaten the wires.*

| newspaper | packet | wires | leaf | plant | cheese |

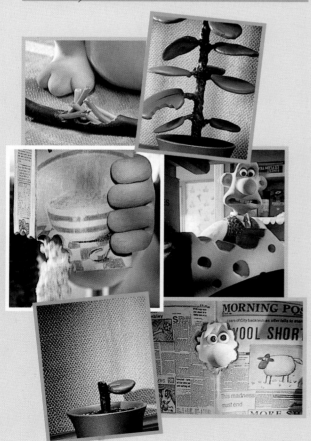

> **See: Grammar, page 12**

Before you watch

1 What does 'wool shortage' mean?

A   Clothes made of wool aren't popular at the moment.

B   There is not enough wool in the shops.

C   The best wool is from small sheep.

While you watch

Slippers
Breakfast
Newspaper
Walkies

2 What happens next? Number these words in order from 1 to 6.

☐ lever

☐ sleeves

☐ porridge

☐ spoon

☐ trousers

☐ pullover

 Watch section two.

After you watch

3 **Write the sentences on the correct pictures.**

- Geronimo!
- Is there a mouse in the house?
- Porridge today, Gromit. Tuesday.
- Turn it off!

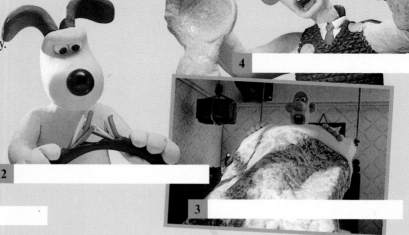

4 _____

2 _____

1 _____

3 _____

 SECTION THREE 02.51 **TO** 04.18

While you watch

1 **What does Wallace say? Tick (✔) the correct answers.**

1 I'm going to make (◯ myself ◯ mine ◯ my own) porridge.
2 (◯ Have ◯ Has ◯ Had) you eaten my cheese, Gromit?
3 Because I haven't had (◯ many ◯ much ◯ any).
4 Something's (◯ eating ◯ eaten ◯ eat) my newspaper.

 Watch section three.

After you watch

2 **Complete the conversation.**

Wallace Hello? Wallace and Gromit's Wash and Go Window Cleaning Service. _____ we help you?

Woman Hello? Um … This is the _____ shop in the High Street. My _____ are very dirty. _____ you clean them today?

Wallace We're on _____ way, madam.

 6

SECTION FOUR 04.19 TO 05.16

While you watch

1 Which of the words do you hear in section four? Tick (✔) the boxes.

boots   pillow   helmet   bucket   washing powder   sponge

hear	○	○	○	○	○	○
see	○	○	○	○	○	○

overalls   motorbike   starter   sidecar   vacuum cleaner   ladder

hear	○	○	○	○	○	○
see	○	○	○	○	○	○

📺 Watch section four.

After you watch

2 Which of the things did you see in section four? Tick (✔) the boxes.

📺 Watch all of episode one again.

3 Now you have finished episode one, ask and answer the questions below the pictures.

Have you seen this dog before?
If yes …
Where did you see him?
Has Gromit seen this dog before?

Has Wallace seen the sheep?
Has Gromit seen the sheep?

Exercises

1 Memory

Are these sentences true (✔) or false (✗)?

1 Gromit was asleep at 2 a.m. ◯
2 Wallace and Gromit are window cleaners. ◯
3 The lorry driver was a man. ◯
4 There was a problem with the porridge machine. ◯
5 The sheep wasn't hungry. ◯
6 A woman telephoned Wallace. ◯
7 Gromit drove the motorbike. ◯
8 The wool shop is in the High Street. ◯

Now correct the false sentences.

2 Test yourself

Choose the correct word in (brackets).

1 Wallace (want / wants) his breakfast.
2 And (much / more) porridge!
3 I'm going (to make / make) my own porridge.
4 Something (has / have) eaten the cheese too.
5 Have you eaten (me / my) cheese, Gromit?
6 Is there a mouse (of / in) the house?
7 What (are / can) you smell, Gromit?
8 My (window's / windows) are very dirty.

Now check with the transcript on page 13

3 is or has or possessive?

Gromit's knitting = Gromit **is** knitting

Gromit's heard something = Gromit **has** heard something

Gromit's wool is red = possessive

What does 's mean in these sentences?
Write is, has or poss. (possessive).

1 Something's eaten the leaf.
2 There's a hole in the newspaper.
3 It's Wallace's newspaper.
4 What's wrong with it?
5 Something's eaten the cheese.
6 That's the problem.

4 Something's eaten (it). Make sentences.
e.g.

There's a hole in the <u>paper</u>.
Something has eaten it.

<u>The biscuits</u> aren't here!
Something has eaten them.

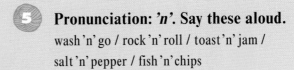

1 What's wrong with the wires?
2 There's a hole in the packet.
3 Look at these leaves!
4 Where's the plant?
5 What's wrong with my boots?

5 Pronunciation: 'n'. Say these aloud.

wash 'n' go / rock 'n' roll / toast 'n' jam /
salt 'n' pepper / fish 'n' chips

6 Sounds. There are two words in each box with a different sound. <u>Underline</u> them.

iː				
sleeve	street	eaten	leaf	breakfast
tea	lever	smell	clean	cheese

aʊ				
house	mouse	down	own	trousers
noise	round			

ɒ				
stopped	clock	lorry	porridge	going
problem	wrong	wool		

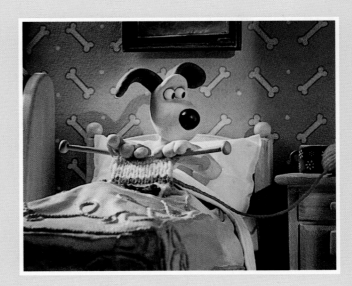

8

Transfer

1 Breakfast. Match the words with the pictures.

Monday: Bacon & egg
Tuesday: Porridge
Wednesday: Toast & jam
Thursday: Cornflakes
Friday: Kippers
Saturday: Boiled egg
Sunday: Cheese on toast

2 Work with a partner. Ask and answer questions.

 What does he have for breakfast on Monday?

He has bacon and egg on Monday.

3 Work with a partner. Ask and answer questions about breakfast, lunch and dinner.

drink	tea	coffee	water	milk	orange juice
	hot chocolate				
food	eggs	toast	bread	jam	cheese
	fruit	porridge	fish	potatoes	
	pasta	a sandwich	soup	pizza	
	a hamburger	a croissant	meat		

 What did you have for breakfast this morning?

I had a croissant and orange juice.

See: Grammar, page 12, Past simple

4 Have you eaten … ? Ask and answer questions with words from the boxes.

been	on a motorbike	in a plane	on a ship
	on a train	in a balloon	
eaten	porridge	kippers	English cheese
	fish 'n' chips		

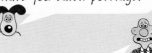 Have you eaten porridge?

Yes, I have. / No, I haven't.

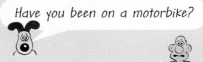 Have you been on a motorbike?

Yes, I have. / No, I haven't.

5 Change partners. Ask and answer questions about your new partner's first partner.

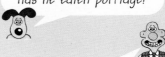 Has he eaten porridge?

Yes, he has. / No, he hasn't.

 Has she been on a motorbike?

Yes, she has. / No, she hasn't.

See: Grammar, page 12, Present perfect

Vocabulary

1 **Window cleaning service**
Read this. Look at the bold words. Put them in the correct boxes on the picture.

Wallace and Gromit are window cleaners. Wallace is on the **motorbike**, and Gromit's in the **sidecar**. There's a **ladder** on the sidecar. They're both wearing **helmets**. Gromit has a pair of goggles on his helmet. Wallace is wearing blue **overalls** and **boots**. The bucket and sponge are in the sidecar. You can't see them.

2 **A bowl of porridge. Match words from column A and column B.**
e.g.
a bowl of porridge

Column A		Column B
a bowl	of	tea
a pair		water
a cup		slippers
a ball		wool
a bucket		porridge

3 **The phone call. Underline the words you don't know in the text.**

Wallace is on the phone. The owner of the wool shop in the High Street has just called him because she wants him to clean her windows. Wallace is sitting in his armchair. Wallace's feet are on the sheep, but Wallace hasn't seen the sheep. He thinks his feet are on the pouffe. He isn't wearing socks or slippers. The sheep is eating the stuffing from the pouffe. The stuffing is straw. The sheep has already eaten Wallace's newspaper. There's a hole in it.

Compare your underlined words with a partner's. Can you guess their meaning?

10

4 Observation. Which of these signs did you see in episode one?

PUSH

GO

STOP

Wendolene's Wools

PULL

ON
OFF

SERVICE

WAL1

5 Vocabulary notebook
Write translations. You can use your dictionary.

1)	asleep	mouse	25)
2)	away	noise	26)
3)	boots	open(ed)	27)
4)	bucket	overalls	28)
5)	cheese	packet	29)
6)	cheese knife	plant	30)
7)	clean(ing)	porridge	31)
8)	close(d)	pouffe	32)
9)	corner	problem	33)
10)	dirty	pullover	34)
11)	down	round	35)
12)	drain	sheep	36)
13)	drive / drove	shop	37)
		sleeves	38)
14)	eat / eaten	smell	39)
		sponge	40)
15)	footsteps	spoon	41)
16)	helmet	starter	42)
17)	hole	stop	43)
18)	house	traffic-lights	44)
19)	knit(ting)	trousers	45)
20)	ladder	up	46)
21)	leaf	windows	47)
22)	lever	wires	48)
23)	lorry	wool	49)
24	motorbike	wrong	50)

11

Grammar

1 Past simple: regular verbs

I	opened	the door.
You	closed	the window.
She	cleaned	
He		
We		
They		

I	didn't /	open	the door.
You	did not	close	the window.
She		clean	
He			
We			
They			

Did	you	open	the door?
	we	close	the window?
	they	clean	
	she		
	he		
	I		

Yes, I did. / Yes, she did. / Yes, they did.
No, you didn't. / No, he didn't. / No, they didn't.

What did you have for breakfast?
I had porridge and tea.

2 Past simple: regular verbs, spelling

+ ed: open / opened, clean / cleaned, turn / turned
+ d: close / closed
double the letter + ed: stop / stopped

3 I, me, my

Subject pronoun	I	you	he	she	it	we	they
Object pronoun	me	you	him	her	it	us	them
Possessive adjective	my	your	his	her	its	our	their

4 Present perfect

I	've /	eaten	the cheese.
You	have		
We	haven't		
They			
She	's /		
He	has		
It	hasn't		

Have	you	eaten	the cheese?
	we		
	they		
	I		
Has	she		
	he		
	it		

Yes, I have. / Yes, she has.
No, we haven't. / No, he hasn't.

5 *Something has eaten it!*

Something has eaten the leaf. /
    Something has eaten it.
Something has eaten the wires. /
    Something has eaten them.

6 *can / can't*

What can you smell?
Can I help you?
Can you clean them today?

Transcript

SECTION ONE

Narrator It was two o'clock in the morning but Gromit wasn't asleep. He heard a noise. It was a lorry. It stopped at the traffic-lights. Gromit heard a sheep. Then he heard footsteps. A door opened. And closed again. The traffic-lights turned green. And the lorry drove away.

SECTION TWO

Narrator Episode one, The uninvited guest.

A nice cup of tea and the morning paper. Uh, oh. Wallace wants his breakfast.

Wallace Porridge today, Gromit. Tuesday.

Narrator Lever …

Wallace Geronimo!

Narrator Trousers … sleeves … pullover … spoon … and, porridge.

Wallace Uh? Uh?

Narrator And more porridge …

Wallace Ow! Ow!

Narrator … and more, and more.

Wallace Turn it off, Gromit! Ow. Off!

Narrator What's wrong with it, Gromit? That was easy. Ah, that's the problem.

Wallace Is there a mouse in the house?

SECTION THREE

Narrator What's that?

Wallace I'm going to make my own porridge.

Narrator Something has eaten the leaf.

Wallace Well, look at that!

Narrator And the packet. Something has eaten the cheese too.

Wallace Have you eaten my cheese, Gromit? Because I haven't had any.

Narrator Something has eaten the plant. It's round the corner. What can you smell, Gromit?

Wallace Huh. Something's eaten my newspaper. There's a hole in it.

Hello? Wallace and Gromit's Wash and Go Window Cleaning Service. Can we help you?

Wendolene Hello? Um … This is the wool shop in the High Street. My windows are very dirty. Can you clean them today?

Wallace We're on our way, madam.

SECTION FOUR

Narrator Up. And down. Boots on. Helmet on. Bucket and sponge. Overalls. Motorbike. And Gromit. Door open. Ladder. Starter. And away!

Uh, oh!

Love at first sight

Watching the video

SECTION ONE 00.00 TO 00.39

Before you watch

1 What do you remember?

Where were they?
Is the one with the ring married or single?

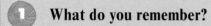 Watch all of episode two.

After you watch

2 Whose are they? Use the names in the box. Ask and answer questions.

Wallace	Gromit	Wendolene	Preston

e.g.

Whose collar is it?

It's Preston's collar.

Kubiwa

helmet

collar

ring

bone

tie

father

See: Grammar, page 22, *Whose?* / possessive *'s*

Before you watch

Seikakuna
Tadashii teigi

1 Choose the correct definition.

bungee /'bʌndʒɪ/ *n* something you tie around yourself, like a belt. A safety harness. **bungee-jumping** working while tied to a safety harness to prevent accidents.

bungee /'bʌndʒɪ/ n a strong elastic rope made of rubber. **bungee-jumping** jumping from a high place, e.g. a bridge, while tied to a bungee. You then bounce up and down.

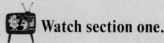 Watch section one.

After you watch

2 Correct the mistakes in this text.

Wallace was inside the wool shop. He saw Wendolene through the shop door. Wendolene saw Gromit. Wallace waved to her first, then she waved back to him. Furu

3 Ask and answer questions.

What does Gromit need?
What colour does he need?

SECTION TWO 00.40 TO 01.45

Before you watch

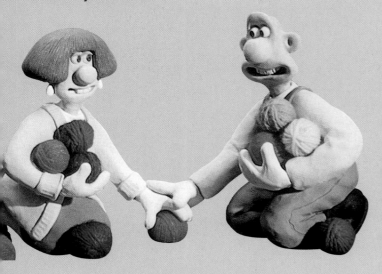

1 Who says it? Write WAL for Wallace, or WEN for Wendolene.

1 Thank you for coming today.
2 Don't worry. とりに行く
3 I can pick them all up.
4 It's no problem.
5 Let me help you.
6 What was it you wanted?

While you watch

2 Check your answers.

📺 Watch section two.

belt おび

Safely あんぜん 使いこなす
 harness)

to prevent ふせぐ 防ぐ
accidents じこ 事故 tanoshimasery

After you watch

3 Did you see this sign? What does it mean?

ウール yama はいきゅうりょう
→Haikyūryō

WOOL RATIONING

TWO BALLS PER PERSON

不足 Fwoku.

A Customers cannot buy one ball of wool. They must buy two.

B Customers pay less if they buy two balls of wool.

C There is a wool shortage. Each customer can buy one or two balls of wool, but cannot buy more.

4 Choose the correct words.

1 Wallace looks (shy / confident).

2 Wallace looks (pleased / embarrassed).

3 Wendolene looks (surprised / amused).

4 Wallace (knows / doesn't know) what to say.

▶ **See:** Grammar, page 22, *look(s)* + adjective

15

SECTION THREE · 01.46 TO 02.55

Before you watch

1 **What does 'rustling' mean?**

A   making a noise

B   stealing sheep or cows

C   escaping

While you watch

2 **Who says it? Write WAL for Wallace, or WEN for Wendolene.**

1   Lovely name.

2   Is this place yours?

3   He was an inventor.

4   I'm an inventor myself.

5   Your dog's waiting.

6   The bounce has gone from his bungee.

7   They're shining.

8   You've done a lovely job.

9   Windows are our speciality.

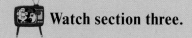 **Watch section three.**

After you watch

3 **Ask and answer questions.**

Who is the man in the picture?

Is he dead or alive?

When did he leave the shop to Wendolene?

Did he leave her any money?

What else did he leave her?

What was her father's job?

4 **Choose the correct words.**

The police	haven't	fought	this	sheep rustlers	then.
	didn't	caught	these		yet.
	hasn't	bought	those		

But	you	got	a lot of	wool,	today.
Yet	you've	get	a shop of	lots of	eh?
	you'd	bought			

5 **Look at 4. What does Wendolene do when Wallace says these things? Tick (✔) the correct sentences.**

She looks guilty. ○

She smiles. ○

She changes the subject (She talks about something different.) ○

She agrees with him. ○

She doesn't answer Wallace. ○

16

SECTION FOUR 02.56 TO 04.06

Before you watch

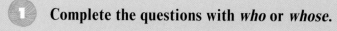

1 Complete the questions with *who* or *whose*.

_____ shadow is this?

_____ is hiding?

_____ has done this?

_____ bone is it?

_____ is eating it?

While you watch

2 Find the answers to the questions in 1.

Watch section four.

After you watch

3 Complete the questions with *what*, *where* or *who*.

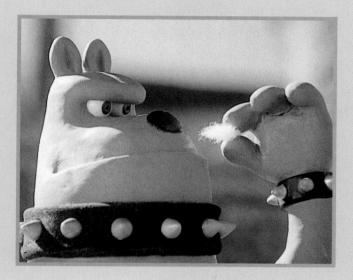

1 _____ is this? It's Preston.

2 _____ has Preston found?

3 He's found some wool.

4 _____ did Preston find it?

5 He found it in the dog flap.

4 What did Wallace say? Tick (✔) the correct words.

1 (◯ Let's / ◯ Let) have a nice cup of tea.

2 Good grief! What (◯ a / ◯ the) mess.

3 (◯ Burglars / ◯ Rustlers), do you think?

4 I (◯ don't / ◯ can't) believe it, Gromit.

5 The poor little lad's (◯ angry / ◯ hungry).

6 Come here, chuck. Don't (◯ be / ◯ feel) sheepish.

7 (◯ You'd like / ◯ You need) a good wash.

 Watch all of episode two again.

17

Exercises

1 **Memory**
Are these sentences true (✔) or false (✗)?

1   Preston lives in West Wallaby Street.
2   Wendolene likes knitting.
3   Gromit needed a ball of blue wool.
4   Wendolene's father left her some money.
5   Wendolene's father was a window cleaner.
6   Preston grabbed Gromit by the neck.
7   The room was in a mess.
8   Preston made the mess.

Now correct the false sentences.

2 **Test yourself**
Choose the correct word in (brackets).

1   Thank you for (come / coming) today.
2   I can pick (them / they) all up.
3   Let (me / I) help you.
4   My father (left / leave) it to me when he died.
5   He needs (me / my) help.
6   Wallace and Gromit (lives / live) there.
7   What did you (hear / heard), Gromit?
8   Go with (them / they), Gromit!

Now check with the transcript on page 23.

3 **What are they doing? Make sentences about the pictures. Use verbs from the box.**

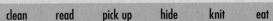

| clean | read | pick up | hide | knit | eat |

4 **Make these sentences negative.**
e.g.

He left Wendolene some money.
He didn't leave Wendolene any money.

1   The rustlers caught some sheep.
2   They had a cup of tea.
3   Preston picked up some wool.
4   Wallace cleaned the window.
5   Wallace heard a noise.

5 **Make the sentences in 4 into questions.**
e.g.

He left Wendolene some money.
Did he leave Wendolene any money?

> **See:** Grammar, page 22, Past simple: irregular verbs

6 **Sounds**
Find the word in each line with a different vowel sound.
e.g.

Line 1: The different word is *wool*.

1	poor	wool	for	door
2	bone	done	phone	own
3	house	mouse	bounce	yours
4	burglar	bungee	hungry	jump
5	leave	believe	nice	grief
6	gone	wash	worry	job

> **See:** Grammar, page 22, Present continuous

Transfer

1 Ask and answer questions around the class.

> What's your first name?

> Wendolene.

> Nice to meet you, Wendolene. What's your last name?

> Ramsbottom.

> Have you got a middle name?

> No, I haven't. / Yes, it's ...

2 What do you like doing? Ask and answer questions around the class. Use words from the box, or add your own ideas.

sports, etc.	playing (tennis) running dancing doing (karate) walking
at home	watching TV listening to music knitting playing computer games surfing the Internet
outside	going to the cinema shopping meeting friends

e.g

> What do you like doing in your free time?

> I like knitting. What about you?

> I like inventing things.

3 Change partners. Ask and answer questions about your new partner's first partner.

> What does Gromit like doing in his free time?

> He likes knitting. What about Preston?

> He likes reading the newspaper.

4 Wallace isn't very good at starting a conversation. Here are some ideas for starting a conversation. Match the questions and answers below.

Question	Answer
1 Where do you live?	A Yes, please.
2 Are you married?	B No, I'm an only child.
3 Would you like (a cup of tea)?	C Upstairs. Over the shop.
4 What do you do?	D Yes, I do.
5 Have you got any brothers or sisters?	E I work in a shop.
6 Do you like (knitting)?	F No, I'm single.

5 Ask your partner the questions in 4.

6 Change partners. Ask and answer questions about your new partner's first partner.

19

Vocabulary

1 **What has the sheep eaten? Tick (✔) the words.**

picture ◯ mirror ◯ vase ◯ clock ◯ magazine ◯ carpet ◯ pouffe ◯ fireplace ◯

electric fire ◯ cushion ◯ armchair ◯

2 **Wordplay**

Wendolene This isn't a real name. It sounds like 'Gwendolene' which is a real name. It's a wordplay on 'Windolene' which is a famous British window-cleaning liquid.

Ramsbottom Family names ending with -bottom are common in the North of England. 'bottom' is the floor of a valley. A *ram* is a male sheep. So Ramsbottom means a valley with sheep in it. It's a place name.

'The Telegruff' *The Daily Telegraph* is a British newspaper. 'gruff' is a noise a dog might make.

sheepish means feeling embarrassed because you've done something silly. Wallace feels *sheepish* after the balls of wool fall down. It's a play on words when Wallace says it to the sheep.

3 ***boy, lad, chuck.* Make true sentences.**

Wallace	calls	Preston	boy.
		the sheep	lad.
			chuck.

Note: *boy* and *lad* are the same.

chuck is a friendly expression from the North of England. It's the same as *dear* or *love*.

20

4 Things you can knit. Write the words under the pictures.

cardigan	sleeveless pullover	socks	hat
gloves	scarf	jumper	

5 Vocabulary notebook
Write translations. You can use your dictionary.

1 _____

2 _____

3 _____

4 _____

5 _____

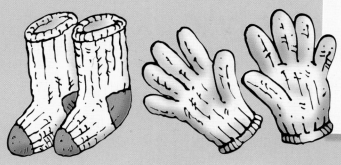

6 _____   7 _____

believe しんじる 信じる

bone ほね けつい 骨 死体

bounce はずむ

boy 男 小生

bungee せん 木全

burglar どろどう 強盗

catch / caught ～ち つかまえる

clever りこうな 利口な

die / died 死ぬ

father ちちおや 父親

go / went / gone 行く 行った 去った (×)

Good grief! それ それでしょう

hide ほ覚す(かく)

hungry 空月貢 くうふう

inventor はつめが 発明家

job 仕事

jump はねる

lad 若者

leave / left 去る (×3)

live 生きる ⑤

(a) lot of たかxんの ㉟

lovely 美しい ⑥

mess xくらん けた じょうた

money 金 ⑦

name 名前

need ひつよう 必要 ⑧

outside タトイ則 (そとがわ) ⑨

pick up のせる ⑩

place ばしょ 場所 ⑫

police 警審官 ⑪

rustler かっていうか うしどろぼう

sheepish うちきな ⑬

shine 光る (ひかる) かがやく ⑭

speciality とくべつに ⑮

think 考える ⑯

wait 待つ ⑰

wash 洗う ⑱

yet まナご ⑲

Grammar

1 Past simple: irregular verbs

He You I She We They	left found got	some money.

He You She He We They	didn't did not	leave find get	any money.

Did	he you we they she I	leave find get	any money?

Yes, I did. / Yes, she did. / Yes, they did.
No, you didn't. / No, he didn't. / No, they didn't.

leave → left
hear → heard
find → found
get → got

2 Present perfect: *yet*

They You We I	haven't	caught found got	the rustlers them	yet.
She He It	hasn't			

Have	they we you I	caught found got	the rustlers them	yet?
Has	she he it			

Yes, they have. / Yes, she has.
No, we haven't. / No, he hasn't.
Do not use *yet* with positive sentences.

3 *do / did / done*

Present	Past	Past participle
do	did	done
go	went	gone
leave	left	left
catch	caught	caught
find	found	found
eat	ate	eaten
get	got	got
clean	cleaned	cleaned

4 Present continuous

Where's Preston going? Your dog's waiting.
Oh, they're shining!   It's eating your bone.

5 *Whose?* / possessive *'s*

Whose shop is it?   It's Wendolene's shop. /
                    It's **her** shop. / It's **hers**.

6 *your / yours*

Your dog's waiting. / Is this place yours?
It's my house. / It's mine.

Possessive adjective	my	your	his	her	our	their
Possessive pronoun	mine	yours	his	hers	ours	theirs

7 *look(s)* + adjective

Is he shy?
I don't know, but he looks shy.
Is she guilty?
I don't know, but she looks guilty.

22

Transcript

SECTION ONE

Narrator Episode two, Love at first sight.

Wallace is outside the wool shop. And Gromit's up the ladder. A bungee jump! That's clever.

Wallace Huh? Oooh. You need wool, Gromit.

SECTION TWO

Wendolene Thank you for coming today.

Wallace Oh, dear!

Wendolene Oh! Don't worry. Please.

Wallace Oh, I'm sorry. Oh … I can pick them all up. It's no problem. I'm sorry.

Wendolene This is Preston. My dog.

Wallace All right, boy? Let me help you.

Wendolene Oh!

Wallace Well …

Wendolene What was it you wanted?

Wallace I … uh … I … uh, mmm, em … I … mm …

Narrator Where's Preston going?

SECTION THREE

Wendolene Ramsbottom. Wendolene Ramsbottom.

Wallace Lovely name. I'm Wallace … the windows? Heh, heh. Is this place yours?

Wendolene Mm. My father left it to me when he died. He didn't leave me any money. Just Preston. He was an inventor.

Wallace Really! Oh, I … I'm an inventor myself. Heh heh.

Wendolene Oh.

Wallace The police haven't caught those sheep rustlers yet. But you've got a lot of wool, eh?

Wendolene Your dog's waiting.

Wallace Yes. He needs my help. The bounce has gone from his bungee.

Wendolene Oh, they're shining! You've done a lovely job.

Wallace Windows are our speciality.

SECTION FOUR

Narrator West Wallaby Street … Wallace and Gromit live there. And here they are. Preston's hiding.

Wallace Let's have a nice cup of tea. Good grief! What a mess! Who's done this? Burglars, do you think?

Narrator What did you hear, Gromit? It's a sheep! It's eating your bone.

Wallace I don't believe it, Gromit. Look at this. Aaah, the poor little lad's hungry. Come here, chuck. Don't be sheepish. You need a good wash.

Narrator Go with them, Gromit!

Watching the video

SECTION ONE 00.00 **TO** 02.04

Before you watch

1 **Ask and answer questions.**

What has Preston got in his hand?

Where did he find it?

Where is the sheep?

Is Preston looking for the sheep?

What's Preston going to do next?

 Watch all of episode three.

After you watch

2 **Look at the pictures. What's going to happen next?**

See: Grammar, page 32, 'going to' future

Before you watch

1 **Number the pictures in order from 1 to 6.**

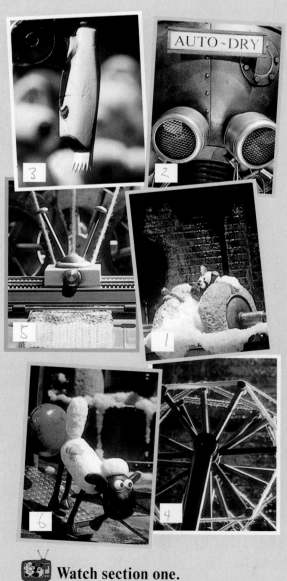

AUTO-DRY

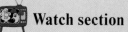 **Watch section one.**

After you watch

2 **What does the Knit-O-Matic do? Match the sentences to the pictures in 1. Put the sentences in order.**

4	It spins the wool.	1	It washes the sheep
2	It dries the sheep.	6	It ejects the sheep.
5	It knits the jumper.	3	It shears the sheep.

> See: Vocabulary, page 30

3 **What went wrong? Complete the sentences.**

Gromit selected [   ], but there was a problem. The machine had a [   ].
It switched itself to [   ].

4 **Complete Wallace's sentences.**

1 Gromit had a wash [   ], didn't you, lad?

2 Right. Let's [   ], then.

3 Lovely jumper. But it's [   ] small for me.

4 He [   ] OK to me.

5 [   ] call him Shaun, eh?

Before you watch

1 **What does the headline mean?**

A Someone has lost a dangerous dog.

B Someone is killing dogs. The person is still free.

C A dog is killing sheep. No one has caught it yet. It is still free.

Watch section two.

After you watch

2 **Complete the spaces with *going to take / taken / taking*.**

Shaun's [   ] the cheese.

Shaun's [   ] the cheese.

Shaun's [   ] the cheese.

> See: Grammar , page 32, *going to do / doing / done*

3 **Ask and answer questions.**

What did Preston take?

What's Shaun wearing?

Why is he wearing it?

When are Wallace and Gromit washing the clock?

SECTION THREE 03.10 TO 04.15

Before you watch

1 **Read this.**

Wallace is an inventor. The gun is one of Wallace's inventions. It can fire porridge or soap.

 Watch section three.

After you watch

2 **Complete the conversation.**

Wendolene Tell me about [   ] .

Wallace Well, it's a temporary [   ] , you understand.

Wendolene Oh, really?

Wallace Oh, yes. I'm an [   ] , you see. Only …

Wendolene Oh, what sort of [   ] ?

Wallace Well, sort of …

Wendolene Daddy [   ] things too. Poor Daddy!

See Vocabulary, page 30, *invent*, etc.

SECTION FOUR 04.15 TO 06.10

Before you watch

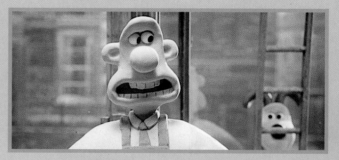

1 **How do they feel? Tick (✔) the sentences you agree with.**

1 Wallace knows that Gromit is watching him. ○
2 Wallace doesn't know that Gromit is watching him. ○
3 Gromit can't hear their conversation. ○
4 Gromit is trying to hear their conversation. ○
5 Gromit is jealous of Wendolene. ○
6 Gromit doesn't like Wendolene. ○
7 Gromit is suspicious of Wendolene and Preston. ○

 Watch section four.

After you watch

2 Look at the box. Complete the sentences.

Gromit's going to ____ the door.

Gromit's ____ the door.

Gromit's ____ the door. But Shaun's ____!

Infinitive	Present participle	Past participle
to open	opening	opened
to go	going	gone
to untie	untying	untied
to close	closing	closed

Gromit's ____ to untie Shaun.

Gromit's ____ Shaun.

Gromit has ____ Shaun.

What's Preston ____ to do? Preston's going to ____ the door.

What is happening? The door is ____

What has happened? The door has ____ Gromit can't escape!

> **See:** Grammar, page 32, *going to do / doing / done*

3 What did Wallace say? Tick (✔) the correct words.

1 Of all the (⬤ women / ⬤ ladies) I've met …
2 I (⬤ haven't / ⬤ have) met many of course.
3 What I'm (⬤ try / ⬤ trying) to say is …
4 This is difficult for (⬤ me / ⬤ my).
5 The (⬤ next / ⬤ same) time next week?

📺 Watch all of episode three again.

After you watch the whole episode

4 Talk about these pictures.

> **See:** Exercises, page 28, 1 Memory

Exercises

1 Memory
Are these sentences true (✔) or false (✗)?

1 Preston watched Shaun in the Knit-O-Matic machine.
2 Gromit saw Preston in the cellar.
3 The soap from the soap gun hit Wallace.
4 Shaun went through the gate next to the shop.
5 The picture of the butcher was behind the hole in the wall.
6 Gromit found a tin of cat food in the room.
7 The sheep didn't go through the shop.
8 Wendolene didn't know that the sheep were in the lorry.

Now correct the false sentences.

2 Test yourself
Choose the correct word in (brackets).

1 It works very (well / good).
2 Lovely jumper. But it's (too / very) small for me.
3 He looks (very / a bit) cold.
4 What does he (wants / want)?
5 Wallace has (shut / shutting) the door.
6 Preston's at the window (then / again)
7 How did Shaun (get / go) up there?
8 Who (takes / took) that photograph?

Now check with the transcript on page 33.

3 Complete the sentences with *much* or *many*.

1 There was too _____ soap.
2 How _____ sheep were there?
3 There isn't _____ time! We're late.
4 How _____ wool was there in the shop?
5 Wallace hasn't met _____ women.

4 Complete the sentences with *too* or *very*.

1 Hurry! We're _____ late. The bus leaves in two minutes.
2 Oh, no! The bus has gone. We were _____ late.
3 Ow! I can't drink this coffee. It's _____ hot for me!
4 It's a lovely day. It's _____ hot.
5 There's _____ much sugar in this tea. I can't drink it.

5 Match the words with the same vowel sound.
e.g. *took / wool*

| same | soap | took | met | clock | turn | loose |
| too | wool | escape | works | job | let's | closed |

6 Stress. Which is the stressed sound in these words?
e.g.

in-ven-tion

ven is the stressed sound.

1 ma-chine
2 jump-er
3 prob-lem
4 tak-en
5 tem-por-ary

6 pho-to-graph
7 dif-fi-cult
8 es-cape
9 bu-tcher
10 wo-men

28

Transfer

1 **What are you going to do? Ask and answer questions with a partner.**

What are you going to do on Saturday?

I'm going to clean my motorbike. What about you?

I'm going to knit a scarf for Preston.

Continue.

What are you going to do after this lesson?

What are you going to do tonight?

What are you going to do at the weekend?

2 **Change partners. Ask and answer about your new partner's first partner.**

What's Preston going to do on Saturday?

He's going to go for a drive in the country.

Continue.

What is (she / he) going to do after this lesson?

3 **Suggestions. Ask and answer questions about the adverts.**

What are you doing tonight?

I'm staying at home.

Let's go to Nick's Café. Let's have a nice cup of tea.

4 **Ask and answer questions with a partner. Use the ideas below.**

had dinner / yet

done your homework / yet

spent any money / today

watched TV / today

It's 7.30 now.

Have you had dinner yet?

Yes, I have.

No, I haven't.

When did you have dinner?

When are you going to have dinner?

I had dinner at 6 o'clock.

I'm going to have dinner at 9 o'clock.

NICK'S CAFÉ
'The nicest cup of tea in England'

13 High Street

FOOTBALL MATCH

Blackburn Rovers
v
Wolves

7.30 kick-off

THE EMPIRE CINEMA

'The Rustlers'

starring Rex Gruff (PG)

4.30   6.45   9.00

CHEESE EXHIBITION

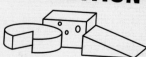

at the Town Hall, Wensleydale
Taste different English cheeses

29

Vocabulary

1 sheep

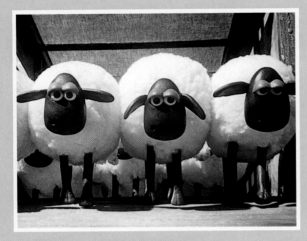

Sheep can be singular (a sheep) or plural (three sheep). A group of sheep is a *flock* of sheep. A young sheep is a *lamb*. A male sheep is a *ram*, and a female sheep is a *ewe* (pronounced like 'you'). The sound a sheep makes is *baa*. We get wool, milk and meat from sheep. Farmers *shear* sheep for their wool. Sheep's milk and sheep's milk cheese wasn't popular in Britain in the past, but it's getting popular now. The meat from sheep is called *lamb* (from young sheep) or *mutton* (from adult sheep). In Britain, *butchers* usually sell *lamb*. *Mutton* isn't very popular.

2 Adjectives ending in *-ous*
Complete the sentence with words from the box.

Shittobukai

nervous	serious	jealous	suspicious

shinkeishitsuna   Utagaibukai

Gromit was _____ because Wallace liked Wendolene.

Gromit was _____ of Wendolene and Preston.

Wallace was very _____ when he was speaking to Wendolene.

Preston never smiles. He always looks _____ .

3 Wordplay

Shaun is also spelled *Sean*. It's a first name in English, e.g. Sean Connery. The pronunciation is the same. The name was originally from Ireland.

shorn sounds exactly the same as Shaun. It's the past participle of the verb *to shear*. Farmers shear sheep when they cut off their wool. If you have a very short haircut, people might say 'Oh! You've been shorn!' So, the machine has shorn Shaun!

a light / close shave *A close shave* is a very careful shave. The machine can give a wash, a light shave or a close shave. Shaun gets a light shave. (Really, the machine *shears* Shaun. It doesn't actually *shave* him.) **a close shave** is also an expression, meaning a narrow escape. If you are crossing the road, and a car misses you by one centimetre, you can say 'That car nearly killed me. That was a close shave!'

'Sud-U-Like' is the name of the soap flakes. You get suds when you mix soap and water. 'U-Like' means **you** like. Compare 'Toys R Us' (Toys **are** Us).

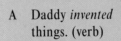
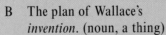

4 to invent, an inventor, an invention

A Daddy *invented* things. (verb)

B The plan of Wallace's *invention*. (noun, a thing)

C I'm an *inventor* (noun, someone who invents; job).

Write A, B or C at the end of these sentences.

There's an art exhibition at the museum. ◯

They're exhibiting some pictures by local artists. ◯

My friend Anna is a painter. She's an exhibitor this week. ◯

5 Use the table. Make true sentences about the pictures.

Wallace	pulled	the	dial.
Gromit	pushed		rope.
	fired		buttons.
	untied		soap-gun.
	turned		lever.

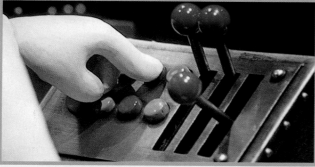

6 Vocabulary notebook
Write translations. You can use your dictionary.

Kawaiteiru

alive iKiteiru
auto-dry ōtomachikku kire? jidō o kawaiteiru
begin
(a) bit
butcher
call
clock
close (adj)
cold
Come on!
come out No sekinin de aru
difficult
escape nigeru
fault Kashitsu (mistake) Keklean
finish
hard(er)
hit Shōtotsu (collision) dāgeki (blow)
inside
invent (v) Hatsumei suru
invention hutsemei hin
jealous Shittobukai
jumper
killer Satsu jin han 'nin
ladies fujin or shukujo
late
machine Kikai

or tasūno
many takusan No
much takusan no nearly ōi ōi? nobō
next week
plan Hippuru?
pull hiku 2 saku (tear)
same
shave Sora Kezuru
shear / shorn
Karitoru
shut tojiru fujikomeru
small Shinaru shimeru
soap
sort (=kind)
suspicious Uta gaib ukai
take / taken
tear / torn yuru
temporary ichiji-tekina
tie up tomeru
tomorrow
try +
understand
untie toKu; hadoKu
well

wren?
refinement?

Grammar

1 going to do / doing / done

He's (is) going to tear the newspaper.

He's (is) tearing the newspaper.

He's (has) torn the newspaper.

I'm going to do it. / I'm doing it. / I've done it.

They're going to eat it. / They're eating it. / They've eaten it.

2 Past participles

Present	Past	Past participle
meet	met	met
shave	shaved	shaved
shear	sheared	shorn
shut	shut	shut
tear	tore	torn
take	took	taken
tie	tied	tied
untie	untied	untied

3 'going to' future

Future intentions with *going to*.

You don't need a time word, *going to (do)* shows that it's future.

I	am / 'm 'm not	going to	have	a wash. dinner.
You We They	are / 're aren't		close	the door. the window.
He She It	is / 's isn't		clean	the clock. the window.

Am	I	going to	have	a wash? dinner?
Are	you we they		close	the door? the window?
Is	he she it		clean	the clock? the window?

4 Present continuous for future arrangements.

The time word shows that it's future

I	am / 'm 'm not	washing cleaning	the clock windows	tomorrow. next week. on Saturday.
You We They	are / 're aren't			
He She It	is / 's isn't			

5 too (= also) / too (late)

1 too (= also)

Daddy invented things too.

She likes knitting. He likes knitting too.

Wallace is a window cleaner. Gromit's a window cleaner, too.

2 too (late)

It's too late now!   It's too small for me.

6 much / many

much goes with <u>uncountable</u> nouns:

How **much** milk is there?

many goes with <u>countable</u> nouns:

How **many** glasses are there?

Wallace: I haven't met **many** women …

Wallace: That was too **much** soap.

7 Suggestions: *let's …*

Let's begin.   Let's call him Shaun.

Transcript

SECTION ONE

Narrator Episode three, The Knit-O-Matic.

Wallace You're going to have a wash, in my new machine. It works very well. Gromit had a wash yesterday, didn't you, lad?

Narrator And Gromit didn't like it.

Wallace Right, let's begin, then.

Narrator Uh, oh. There's a problem. Don't hit it, Gromit.

Wallace Oh, dear. Oh! Do something, Gromit. Oh, it's too late now. Oh! Turn it off, Gromit. Oh, oh … oh, oh. Oh, dear. I can't see. Ah. Lovely jumper! But it's too small for me. Heh heh.

Sheep Baaa!

Narrator He's alive!

Sheep Baa.

Wallace Ha, he looks OK to me.

Narrator He looks a bit cold.

Wallace Let's call him Shaun, eh? Hmm. Come on, Shaun.

SECTION TWO

Narrator Preston's coming out. What does he want? Ah! He wants the plan of Wallace's invention!

Narrator Killer dog on loose … mm. Shaun's torn the newspaper. And he's taken the cheese.

Wallace Er, Gromit? You know we're washing the clock tomorrow.

SECTION THREE

Wallace Sorry, Gromit. That was too much soap. Finish the clock, Gromit. I'm going to the wool shop. Hello, Wendolene …

Narrator Wallace has shut the door. Preston's at the window again. And where's Shaun going?

Wendolene Tell me about windows.

Wallace Well, it's a temporary job, you understand.

Wendolene Oh, really?

Wallace Oh, yes. I'm an inventor, you see. Only …

Wendolene Oh, what sort of inventions?

Wallace Well, sort of …

Wendolene Daddy invented things too. Poor Daddy!

SECTION FOUR

Shaun Baaa. Baaa.

Narrator How did Shaun get up there? What's inside? Who took that photograph?

Wallace Of all the women I've met … er, er … I haven't met many, of course …

Narrator Shaun's gone! Preston's Dog Food? And a picture of a butcher. That's Shaun! He's in the lorry.

Wallace So you see … What I'm trying to say … is … this is difficult for me … er …

Narrator Pull it harder, Gromit! Yes! Uh, oh.

Wallace … ladies I've met … you … Oh. Ah. Ow. The same time next week?

Narrator Shaun's tied up! He can't escape. Untie him, Gromit. The door's closing. Too late! It's closed!

33

Crime and punishment

Watching the video

1 The story so far. Complete the sentences with *Wallace, Gromit, Shaun, Preston* or *Wendolene.*

Episode 1: The uninvited guest

[＿＿＿] was still awake. He was knitting when a lorry stopped outside. [＿＿＿] escaped from the lorry and went into [＿＿＿]'s house. [＿＿＿] was driving the lorry, and [＿＿＿] was with him. [＿＿＿] wanted to catch [＿＿＿], but [＿＿＿] stopped him. The next day, [＿＿＿] phoned [＿＿＿]. She asked [＿＿＿] to clean her windows.

Episode 2: Love at first sight

[＿＿＿] met [＿＿＿] for the first time, and it was love at first sight. There was a wool shortage because of sheep rustlers but [＿＿＿]'s shop had a lot of wool. [＿＿＿] went to [＿＿＿]'s house and hid in the cellar. When [＿＿＿] and [＿＿＿] arrived home, the house was in a mess. [＿＿＿] was in the kitchen.

Episode 3: The Knit-O-Matic

[＿＿＿] took the plan of the Knit-O-Matic. Someone took a photograph of [＿＿＿] and [＿＿＿]. [＿＿＿] went into the room, but [＿＿＿] wasn't there. [＿＿＿] found a tin of [＿＿＿]'s Dog Food. Then he heard [＿＿＿]. He was in the lorry! [＿＿＿] rescued [＿＿＿], but the lorry drove away with [＿＿＿] inside.

 Watch all of episode four.

After you watch

2 Ask and answer questions about the pictures.

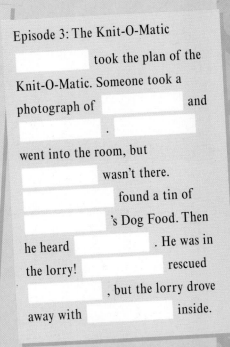

1 Why is she crying?

2 What's in the parcel?

3 Who's in prison?

4 What's going to happen next?

5 Who has Wallace just seen?

6 Who has just hit Preston?

SECTION ONE 00.00 TO 01.06

Before you watch

1 Are these sentences true (✔) or false (✗)?

1 The police have arrested Gromit. ○ たいほ する
2 Gromit murdered a sheep. ○ ころす
3 Gromit's head is in the photograph. ○
4 Gromit's body is in the photograph. ○
5 The photograph is a fake. ○ にせもの
6 Wallace believes that Gromit is guilty. ○ ゆうざい

 Watch section one.

After you watch

2 What did Wendolene say?
e.g.

this / I'm / about / sorry
I'm sorry about this.

1 me / just / away / stay / from
2 no / you / for / good / I'm
3 Gromit / I'm / about / sorry / so

SECTION TWO 01.06 TO 01.55

Before you watch

1 Match the newspapers to the headlines.

 Watch section two.

After you watch

2 Complete the sentences with words from the box.

見出し

jury

jury=baishin'in

| trial | guilty | shepherd | life | headlines |

The newspaper ▭ tell the story
of Gromit's ▭. The dog that killed the
sheep also bit the ▭. At the end of
the trial, the jury decided that Gromit was
▭ of killing the sheep. The judge gave
Gromit '▭ in prison'.

> **See:** Vocabulary, page 40, Wordplay

SECTION THREE 01.55 TO 03.14

Before you watch

1 **What is the message?**

While you watch

2 **Number the pictures in order from 1 to 9.**

 Watch section three.

After you watch

3 **Make true sentences.**

Gromit	was reading	when	the parcel	arrived.
	was in his cell		his dinner	
	didn't get up			
	got up			

Gromit	was	interested	when	he	saw	his dinner.
	wasn't	excited			read	the parcel.
		disappointed				the jigsaw puzzle.
		sad				the message.
		happy				the date and time.
						Shaun.

4 **Find the correct sentence.**

It's	gone.	He's	sawn	a few of	the bars.
He's	Shaun.	It's	torn	through	
Here's	come.		Shaun	two of	

5 **Complete the sentences with words from the box.**

| top | through | above | down | bottom |

When Gromit climbed _____ the window,
he was high _____ the ground. The sheep
were standing on top of one another in a tall
column. Wallace was at the _____ and
Shaun was at the _____. Then Wallace slipped
on the soap, and they all fell _____.

6 **Work with a partner and tell the story of section three.**

SECTION FOUR 03.14 TO 04.45

While you watch

1 Tick (✔) the noises you hear in section four.

a police-car siren ◯
an aeroplane ◯
sheep baaing ◯
dogs barking ◯
a lorry engine ◯
a gate breaking ◯
a lorry stopping ◯
a door opening ◯
a door closing ◯
a whistle ◯
Shaun's teeth chattering ◯
growling ◯
laughing ◯
a shepherd's crook breaking ◯
Wendolene shouting, 'Help'. ◯
a motorbike engine ◯

 Watch section four.

After you watch

2 Check with a partner.

> Did you hear a whistle?

> Yes, I did. / No, I didn't.

3 What did Wallace say? Find the correct sentence.

You	'll	had	to	live in	quickly	though.
I	will	have		believe	the country	now.
We	'd	must		leave	in front	and go.

4 What do you know about the rustlers? Tick (✔) the sentences you agree with.

1 At first, they stole the sheep for their wool. ◯
2 They don't want the wool now. ◯
3 They're going to turn the sheep into dog food. ◯
4 Wendolene wants to stop doing this. ◯
5 The rustling was Preston's idea. ◯
6 Wendolene's father invented Preston. ◯
7 Preston was made to protect her. ◯
8 Preston's going to turn Wendolene into dog food. ◯

5 Work with a partner and tell the story of section four from the pictures.

 Watch all of episode four again.

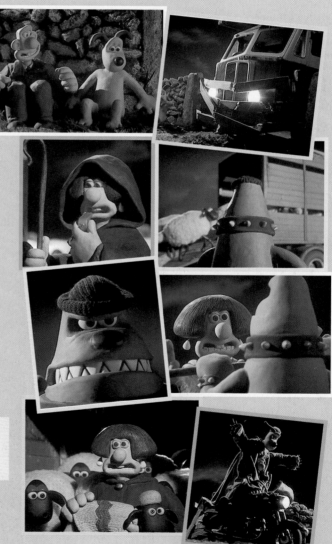

See: Vocabulary, page 41

Exercises

1 Memory
Are these sentences true (✔) or false (✗)?

1 Gromit bit a shepherd.

2 The sheep are living in Wallace's house.

3 Gromit got ten years in prison.

4 Gromit was reading a newspaper in prison.

5 Preston sent the jigsaw puzzle.

6 Shaun sawed through the bars.

7 Wendolene wasn't afraid of Preston.

8 Preston only wanted the wool from the sheep.

9 Wallace is a fugitive from the police.

Now correct the false sentences.

2 Test yourself
Choose the correct word in (brackets).

1 Why did you (done / do) it, lad?

2 There's (something / someone) at the door.

3 It's (any / only a) jigsaw puzzle.

4 (Well done / Welcome), lads.

5 (You'll / You) have to hide.

6 So, (there are / they're) the sheep rustlers!

7 I want (to stop / stopping) this rustling.

8 I'm (on / in) my way!

Now check with the transcript on page 43.

3 Make sentences.
e.g.

Gromit was reading when the parcel arrived.

Gromit was reading	when	he slipped on the soap.
Wallace was reading a newspaper		the lorry crashed through the gate.
Wallace was holding the sheep		Wendolene hit him with her crook.
Preston was growling at Shaun		the parcel arrived.
Wallace and Gromit were sitting in the field		Wendolene rang the doorbell.

4 It's Gromit's first day in prison. Tell him the rules.
e.g.

You'll have to get up at 5 a.m.

PRISON RULES
1 *Get up at 5 a.m.*
2 *Clean your cell.*
3 *Work from 7 to 5.*
4 *Go to bed at 8 p.m.*
5 *Turn off the lights at 8.30*

> **See:** Grammar, page 42, *will have to*

5 Complete the sentences from the video with object pronouns (*me, you, it*).

1 Give _____ back.

2 Just stay away from _____ .

3 Forget _____ .

4 I'm no good for _____ .

5 Daddy didn't invent _____ for this.

6 You were made to protect _____ .

7 Let _____ out.

8 You're not going to turn _____ into dog food.

Now check with the transcript on page 43.

6 Stress. Make sentences about Wallace, Gromit, Wendolene, Preston and Shaun with words from the box. Stress *so*.
e.g. Shaun is <u>so</u> cute.

ugly	English	silly	clever	nice
fierce	unhappy	funny	afraid	cute

7 Sounds. Find the word in each line with a different sound.
e.g. Line 1: The different word is *gone*.

1	Shaun	torn	gone	sawn
2	soap	out	post	so
3	hide	life	trial	give
4	were	leave	evil	seen
5	friend	eight	best	ready
6	stay	same	way	bars

Transfer

1 Who murdered the sheep?

At Gromit's trial, the shepherd said:

'I was sleeping when a noise woke me. I heard a dog. It was growling. I went outside, and my sheep weren't there! Then a dog bit me. I didn't see the dog. It was behind me, and it was a very dark night. Then I found one of my sheep. It was dead. I looked at my watch. It was half past one.'

I was at home at half past one. I was sleeping.

I was awake. I was knitting a scarf.

I was awake. I was knitting a pullover.

I was eating my dinner.

Which ones are telling lies? What were they really doing?

2 Ask and answer questions.

What was Wallace doing?

He was sleeping.

See: grammar, page 42, Past continuous

3 What were you doing at 9 p.m. yesterday evening? Ask and answer questions with a partner.
e.g.

What were you doing at 9 p.m.?

I was at home. I was watching television.

Were you still watching television at ten o'clock?

Yes, I was. / No, I wasn't.

Ask and answer questions about other times.

4 Change partners. Ask and answer questions about your first partner.
e.g.

What was she doing at 9 p.m.?

She was at home. She was watching television.

Was she still watching television at ten o'clock?

Yes, she was. / No, she wasn't.

Vocabulary

1 In prison
**Read this. Look at the bold words. Put
them in the correct boxes on the picture.**

Gromit's in prison. He's sitting on his **bed** in his prison cell. There's a **pillow** on the bed and a **lamp** beside the bed.
There are some **handcuffs** by the lamp. There's a **photo** on the wall, and some **graffiti**.

Gromit's doing a **jigsaw puzzle**. There's a **mug** on the table. There are **bars** on the window.

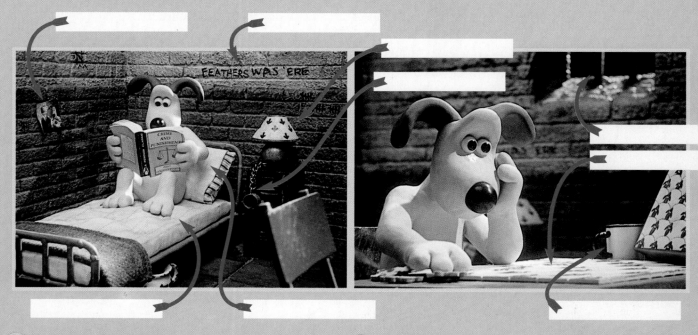

2 **Match words from box 1 with words from
box 2.**
e.g.

jigsaw puzzle

Box 1	Box 2
jigsaw	cell
dog	food
best	lights
prison	friend
traffic	jump
bungee	rustlers
sheep	puzzle

3 Wordplay

'Feathers was ere' is a misspelling of 'Feathers was here'. Feathers McGraw is a penguin who was in Wallace and Gromit's previous adventure, *The Wrong Trousers*. Feathers went to prison at the end of the story.

'Fido Dogstoyevsky' Fyodor Dostoyevsky wrote the Russian novel *Crime and Punishment*. The first name on Gromit's book is 'Fido' which was a popular British name for dogs. The publisher is 'Penguin' with a picture of Feathers McGraw as the logo.

'Sheep Dog Trial' A *sheep-dog* is a type of dog that looks after sheep. Normally a *sheep-dog trial* is a competition between sheep-dogs. These competitions are popular in sheep farming areas. But a *trial* is where a criminal is *tried* by a judge. Both meanings of sheep-dog trial are used here. The newspaper headline 'Sheep Dog Trial ...' means the trial of the dog that killed the sheep, not a sheep-dog.

4 **In the country**
Complete the sentences with words from the boxes.

Kak ashi   Hatake

| scarecrows | field | gate | wall |

mon   Kabe /hei

Wallace and Gromit are sitting in a [____] .
They're sitting against a stone [____] , next to a [____] . There are some [____] in the fields.

hitsujikai o   Kagi   fūdo

| shepherd's crook | hood | whistle |

Wendolene's wearing a coat with a [____] .
She's got a [____] in her right hand and a [____] in her left hand.

| hat | coat | scarecrow |

henjō shite

Wallace and Gromit are disguised as a [____] . Gromit is wearing an old [____] and an old [____] from one of the scarecrows in the next field.

5 **Vocabulary notebook**
Write translations. You can use your dictionary.

prisoner =shūjin

Keimusho

about _____ life (in prison) _____
afternoon _____ make _____
arrest(ed) taiho Suru /Soshi Suru   mind be careful
bars bō /Katamari /Shōgai   morning _____
best _____ nothing Nani mo ... nai
bite Kamitsuki _____ parcel _____
brilliant _____ prison Keimusho ____
continue _____ protect mamoru 守る
country _____ punishment Keibatsu
crime hanzai (o okasu)   puzzle _____
dinner _____ saw / sawed / sawn
evening _____ nokogiri de Kiru ___
evil aku _____ shepherd hitsujikai
fake detchiagery,   silly bakana _____
   nisemono /nise no
forget _____ someone dareka ____
give back _____ stay away chikayoranai
go back _____ through o tōtte _____
guilty yūzai _____ trial Saiban _____
jigsaw jigusō _____ turn into   ni naru
just tatta _____ way   ni iku tochū
leave _____   de

fugitive   on trial
tōbōsha   tameshi ni

                  Stand trial
              Saiban ni Kakerareru

Grammar

1 Imperatives

Give it back.
Stay away from me!
Forget me.
Be ready.
Mind the soap.
Stop it!
Help!
Don't **worry**.

2 Past and past participles

Present	Past	Past participle
give	gave	given
bite	bit	bitten
take	took	taken
saw	sawed	sawn
invent	invented	invented
make	made	made

3 Past continuous

I	was	reading	a book.
He	wasn't	looking at	a letter.
She		writing	
We	were		
You	weren't		
They			

Was	I	reading	a book?
	he	looking at	a letter?
	she	writing	
Were	you		
	they		
	we		

Yes, I was. / No, she wasn't.
Yes, they were. / No, we weren't.

4 when

Gromit was reading **when** his dinner arrived.
Gromit got up **when** the parcel arrived.
Gromit was disappointed **when** he saw the puzzle.
It wasn't so bad **when** we took just the wool.

5 will have to

The future form of *have to* for obligation.

I	'll	have to	leave	the country.
You	will			
He	won't			
She	will not			
It				
We				
They			hide.	

Note: Wallace says, 'You'll have to leave the country now'.

In this sentence *now* isn't a time word. It means 'as a result of your action'.

Will	I	have to	leave	the country?
	you			
	he			
	she			
	it			
	we			
	they		hide?	

6 someone, nothing

There's **someone** at the door.
For what? **Nothing**.

7 two-word verbs

| give back | go back |
| stay away | turn into |

8 so

degree:	conclusion:
I'm so sorry about this.	So, they're the sheep rustlers!
It wasn't so bad.	

9 Expressions

Why did you do it?	Brilliant!
I'm sorry about this.	Well done!
I'm so sorry about (this / Gromit).	Mind (the soap).
I'm no good for you.	Let me out!
(My) best friend.	I'm on my way.

Transcript

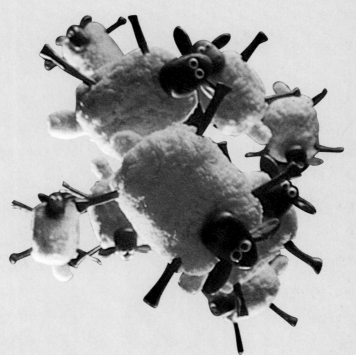

rescue Kyūjo suru
apologise ①ayamaru
②benmei suru

upset - kōfun shitera

SECTION ONE

Narrator Episode four, Crime and punishment. <u>Killer Dog Gromit Arrested</u> ...

Wallace Your photograph in the newspaper. Why did you do it, lad? Hey! Give it back. Shoo! There's someone at the door. Oh ...

Wendolene I'm sorry about this.

Wallace Oh. For what?

Wendolene Nothing. Just stay away from me. From my shop. And my silly, silly windows.

Wallace Well, I ... um ...

Wendolene Forget me. I'm no good for you. I'm so sorry about Gromit.

SECTION TWO

Wallace Owww! Hmmm.

Narrator Morning Post. <u>Sheep Dog Trial Continues</u>.

Wallace Oh, Gromit.

Narrator Afternoon Post. <u>Gromit Bit Me Says Shepherd</u>.

Wallace Oh, Gromit.

Narrator Evening Post. <u>Gromit Gets Life</u>.

Wallace Oh, Gromit! Gromit, my best friend, in prison!

SECTION THREE

Narrator Dinner. And a parcel! It's only a jigsaw puzzle. Friday night! 8 p.m., be ready. A friend. It's Friday! It's eight o'clock. And it's Shaun! He's sawn through the bars.

Wallace Brilliant! Well done, lads! Ha ha. Oooh! Woah!

Narrator Mind the soap!

Wallace Argh. Oooh.

Narrator Too late!

SECTION FOUR

Wallace You'll have to leave the country now. A fugitive, eh? You'll have to hide, or you'll go back to prison.

Wallace Wend ...

Narrator So, they're the sheep rustlers! Preston's seen Shaun.

Preston Grrr.

Wendolene Stop it! Stop it, Preston! Oh. Oh! I want to stop this rustling. It wasn't so bad when we took just the wool, but this is evil. Daddy didn't invent you for this ... Ow! ... You were made to protect me! Let me out! You're not going to turn me into dog food.

Wallace Dog food?

Wendolene Help!

Wallace Don't worry, Wendolene! I'm on my way.

43

Episode 5

No escape

Watching the video

Before you watch

1. **What will happen in episode five? Ask and answer questions.**

   toraeru
   Will Wallace and Gromit catch the lorry?
   tasukeru
   Will they save Wendolene from Preston?

   Will they rescue the sheep?

    Watch all of episode five.

After you watch

2. **Were your ideas correct?**

3. **Work with a partner. Number these pictures in the correct order from 1 to 8.**

SECTION ONE   00.00 TO 00.56

Before you watch

1. **Label the pictures with these words.**

accelerator	barrier	barn	bolt	wires

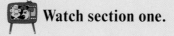

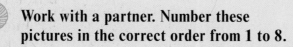 **Watch section one.**

44

After you watch

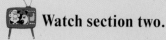

SECTION TWO 00.56 TO 02.01

While you watch

1 **Find answers to these questions.**

1 How many feet is the drop?
2 How many buttons does Gromit push?
3 Who is the first to walk across to the motorbike?
4 Does Wendolene walk across to the motorbike?

Watch section two.

After you watch

2 **Complete the sentences with words from the box.**

in	over	from	behind	up	out
without	ahead	down	past	into	

Wallace thought the lorry was _____ of them, but the lorry was _____ a barn. Wallace went _____ the barn, and the lorry came out of the barn. It was _____ them. The lorry bumped into their motorbike. Gromit climbed _____ the ladder and grabbed the wires. The motorbike went _____ the wires and came _____ . They were behind the lorry. Then the bolt came _____ , and the sidecar separated _____ the motorbike. Gromit was on his own in the sidecar _____ any brakes. The sidecar crashed _____ a barrier.

> **See:** Grammar, page 52, Adverbs of movement.

2 **Match the sentences to the pictures.**

1 Danger! Two-thousand-foot drop.
2 It's turned into a plane!
3 I'll save you.
4 Be careful, Shaun.
5 One at a time, please.
6 You're in the wrong places down there.

SECTION THREE 02.01 to 03.15

Before you watch

1 **Do you know these words?**

fields ◯
goggles ◯
a packet of porridge mix ◯
a bridge ◯
a brake pedal ◯
a mirror ◯
a clock ◯
the moon ◯
clouds ◯
a shop sign ◯
a baker ◯
a lamp-post ◯
chimneys ◯

See: Pictures below; Vocabulary, page 50

While you watch

2 **Tick (✔) the things you see in section three.**

📺 **Watch section three.**

After you watch

3 **Complete the sentences with the verbs in the box. Then put the sentences in the correct order and match them to the pictures.**

stepped   opened   saluted   fired
saw   closed   flew   crashed

☐ Preston _____ the electric window.
☐ Preston _____ the automatic doors.
☐ Wallace _____ the low bridge ahead.
☐ Gromit _____ porridge at the lorry.
☐ The motorbike _____ into the back of the lorry.
☐ Preston _____ on the brake.
☐ Gromit _____ Wallace and the sheep.
☐ Gromit's plane _____ up and over the town clock.

1 2 3 4 5 6 7 8

4 **Work with a partner. Tell the story of section three.**

46

SECTION FOUR 03.15 TO 04.01

Before you watch

1 **Ask and answer questions.**

Who invented the Knit-O-Matic?

Who stole the plans of the invention?

 Watch section four.

After you watch

2 **Choose the best answers.**

1 What's happening?

   A Preston is trying to save them.

   B The tipper car is tipping them into the tub.

   C The tipper car is falling into the tub.

2 What has happened?

   A Shaun has fallen out of the tipper car.

   B Preston has saved Shaun.

   C Everyone's fallen into the tub, except Shaun.

3 What's happening?

   A Wendolene is pushing Wallace into the dryer.

   B Wallace is falling out of the dryer.

   C The dryer is sucking Wallace into the machine.

4 What's Shaun trying to do?

   A He's trying to switch on the neon sign on the chimney.

   B He's trying to switch off the dryer.

   C He's trying to open the factory doors.

5 What has happened?

   A Preston's turned them into dog food.

   B Preston's switched on the neon sign.

   C Shaun's switched on the neon sign.

3 **Watch episode five without sound. Describe to your partner what's happening.**

 Watch all of episode five again.

47

Exercises

1 Memory
Are these sentences true (✔) or false (✗)?

1 Wallace was wearing a red helmet.
2 The bolt came out.
3 The motorbike turned into a plane.
4 Gromit fired soap at the lorry.
5 Gromit saluted Preston.
6 Shaun was driving the motorbike.
7 Gromit nearly crashed into the clock.
8 Wallace escaped from the tipper car.

Now correct the false sentences.

2 Test yourself
Choose the correct word in (brackets).

1 We're at (top / maximum) speed.
2 I can't go (any faster / too fast).
3 Danger! Two-thousand-(foot / feet) drop.
4 Don't (to worry / worry), Wendolene.
5 I ('ll / 'm) save you.
6 You're (in / at) the wrong places down there.
7 Where (did / do) you get that from?
8 You've (stole / stolen) my invention.

Now check with the transcript on page 53.

3 What do the contractions mean? Write *is* or *has* after each sentence.

1 The bolt's loose.
2 It's come out.
3 Gromit's on his own.
4 It's turned into a plane.
5 Gromit's got a gun.
6 Preston's got them.

4 Offer to help someone.
e.g.

Help!
I'll save you!
My windows are dirty.
I'll clean them.

1 It's very hot in here.
2 I'm cold!
3 I need some wool.
4 I'm very thirsty.
5 I'm very hungry.

5 Adjectives are singular. Change the plural nouns into singular adjectives.
e.g.

The flight is seven **hours** long.
*It's a seven-**hour** flight.*

1 The videotape is three hours long.
2 The wall is six feet high.
3 The ruler is thirty centimetres long.
4 The CD is seventy four minutes long.
5 The book is one thousand pages long.

6 Sounds: Past simple of regular verbs
Say the past tenses aloud. What is the sound of *-ed*? Is it /t /, /d / or /ɪd /? Put the verbs in the correct boxes.

climbed bumped grabbed crashed separated
walked turned stepped opened wanted closed
saluted fired tipped pushed needed sucked
switched tried escaped saved

t
d
ɪd

1 Work with a partner. Find the sheep. Where are they? What are they doing?

2 Offer to help your partner. e.g.

 I haven't got a pencil.

 I'll give / lend you my pencil.

 I can't understand this exercise.

 I'll help you.

See: Exercises, page 48

3 Any faster? Practise with a partner.

 You're reading slowly. Can you read faster?

 Sorry. I can't read any faster.

You're walking slowly.

We've walked ten kilometres. Let's walk five more kilometres.

I'm sorry. I'm not ready. Can you wait for half an hour?

Hurry! Run faster! We'll miss the bus!

You're speaking very quietly. Speak louder.

See: Grammar, page 52

Vocabulary

1 Inside the factory
Complete the sentences with words from the box.

| tub | sponges | control panel | rope | dryer | soapy |

Wallace and Wendolene are terrified! They're in a tipper car in the factory, and it's tipping them and the sheep into a _____ of _____ water. There are two large yellow _____ in the tub. Preston is standing at the _____. There's a _____ above him. The rope controls the _____.

2 The plane
Label the picture with these words.

| wing | tail | propeller | cockpit | gun |

3 Match the words in box 1 with their opposites in box 2.
e.g.

ahead – behind

Box 1	Box 2
lost	behind
maximum	slower
faster	found
up	under
wrong	high
without	minimum
low	right
over	with
ahead	down

4 What do these signs mean? Match the signs to the words. Which signs are in episode five?

 1

 4

 2

 5

 3

 6

one way street
no parking
low flying aircraft

road works
maximum speed 30mph
low bridge ahead

5 Pedals

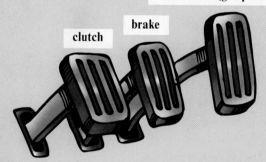

accelerator (gas pedal, USA)
brake
clutch

6 Match words from column 1 and column 2.

Column 1	Column 2
step on	the lever
pull	the switches
push	the brake
turn on	the gun
fire	the button

7 Vocabulary notebook
Write translations. You can use your dictionary.

Go ahead
まっすぐ先に
ahead mae ni/saki ni
bolt boruto//kannuki
brake
bridge
danger
drop rakka?
dryer kansōki (for cloth
faster
fly / flew tobu /sōjū suru
foot (measure) fito
grab tsukamu /toraeru
loose (opp. tight) yurui
lost nakushita / maigono
low

(upper limit)
Saidaigen(no)
maximum Saidai (no)
(highest amount)
pedal
place
plane
over o koete
save tasukeru
speed
steal / stole / stolen nusumu
thousand
tub oke (furo oke)
up
watch out ki o tsukeru
wires harigane/densen
without
Soto de/ni
nashi de

51

Grammar

1 **Adverbs of movement**

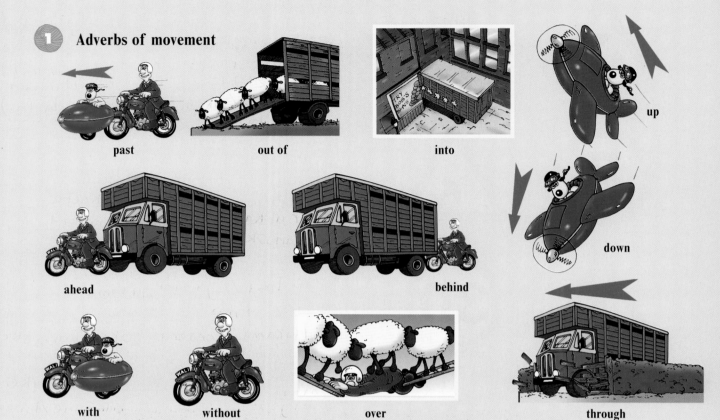

past   out of   into   up

ahead   behind   down

with   without   over   through

2 *I'll save you!*

I	'll /	do	it.
He	will	save	them.
She	won't		
It			
We			
You			
They			

Will	he	do	them?
	she	save	it?
	they		
	you		
	I		
	we		

Yes, (he) will. / No, (she) won't.

3 **Comparative adverbs with: *any***

I can't go any faster.
It's late. I can't wait any longer.
I'm very tired. I can't walk any further.

4 *A two-thousand-foot drop*

The drop is two thousand **feet**.
(*feet* is a plural noun)
It's a two-thousand-**foot** drop.
(*foot* is an adjective. Adjectives are always singular.)
Note: A foot is thirty centimetres.

Compare:

The tape is ninety minutes long.
It's a ninety-minute tape.

5 **Expressions**

maximum speed
on (his) own
One at a time.
Watch out!
Do something!

Transcript

SECTION ONE

Narrator Episode five, No escape.

Wallace Where are they? We've lost them.

Narrator Oh, no, you haven't. They're behind you.

Wallace Ah! Ah! We're at maximum speed. I can't go any faster.

Narrator Up the ladder. Grab the wires. Over …

Wallace Aah! Whoah!

Narrator … and down. Brilliant! Oh, no, the bolt's loose. It's come out. Gromit's on his own … without any brakes.

SECTION TWO

Narrator Danger! Two-thousand-foot drop. It's turned into a plane!

Wendolene Wallace, help me!

Wallace Don't worry, Wendolene. I'll save you. Whoah!

Wendolene Be careful, Shaun.

Wallace One at a time, please. Aah! One at a time, I said. You're in the wrong places down there.

SECTION THREE

Narrator Ah, Gromit's got a gun. And some porridge.

Wallace Huh?

Narrator Low bridge ahead.

Wallace Watch out, lads!

Narrator They're through.

Wallace Oh, no! Aah!

Narrator Preston's got them. But here's Gromit. Watch out. Phew! Gromit's lost them.

SECTION FOUR

Wallace Where did you get that from? That's my machine. You've stolen my invention.

Narrator Into the tub … except Shaun. Oh, no, the dryer!

Wendolene Help. Oh, Shaun. Help!

Wallace Where's Gromit?

Wendolene Shaun, do something. Help!

Narrator Is Preston going to turn them into dog food?

Gromit to the rescue

Watching the video

Before you watch

1 **What's going to happen in episode six?**
Here are some predictions about episode six.
Agree (✔) or disagree (✗).

Preston is going to go to prison. ◯

Wallace is going to get married to Wendolene. ◯

Shaun is going to return to the flock and live in a field. ◯

The police are going to send Wendolene to prison. ◯

Gromit's plane is going to crash. ◯

Gromit's going to rescue everyone. ◯

SECTION ONE 00.00 TO 01.24

 Watch section one.

After you watch

the wooden door   the metal door   the brick wall

1 **Complete the sentences.**

First, Gromit pushed the ▭ button,
and the ▭ went in. He flew through
the ▭ door.

2 **Write about the second door.**

3 **Complete the sentences.**

Third, Gromit didn't ▭ the ▭
button in time. He was too ▭ ! The
wings didn't ▭ in. He flew through the
▭ wall and the ▭ came off.

2 **Have you got any other predictions?**

 Watch all of episode six.

After you watch

3 **Were the predictions right? Correct the wrong ones.**

4 **Number the sentences in order from 1 to 9.**

▭ Preston went through the tube into the Knit-O-Matic.

▭ Shaun pulled the rope and moved the dryer.

▭ Gromit fired porridge at Preston, but one shot missed and hit Wallace in the face.

▭ The plane spun round and Gromit shot out.

▭ Preston caught the propeller and the plane stopped.

▭ Gromit turned the dial to 'close shave' and the machine started to shear Preston.

▭ Gromit landed on a platform.

▭ Wallace fell out of the dryer.

▭ Preston went into the dryer.

5 **Describe what happened. Connect the sentences in 4 with *first, then, next, finally*.**

> **See:** Grammar, page 62, Sequence words

SECTION TWO 01.24 to 02.20

While you watch

1 **Number the pictures in order from 1 to 7.**

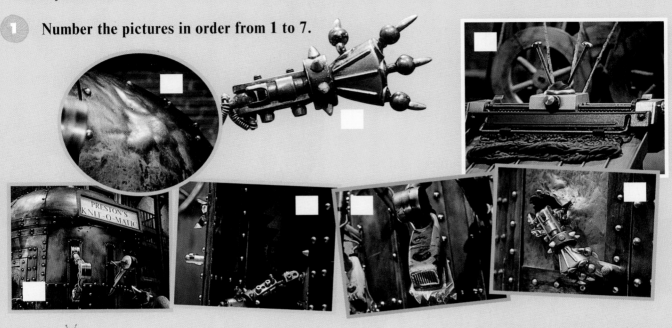

📺 **Watch section two.**

After you watch

2 **Match the sentences to the pictures. Write the numbers of the pictures.**

- Then the machine started knitting a dog hair jumper.
- Preston punched a hole in the machine.
- Next Preston started punching the machine.
- Finally, he opened the door.
- Then he found the door handle and turned it.
- First the Knit-O-Matic started shearing Preston.
- The machine stopped.

3 **What did Wendolene tell Wallace? Correct the mistakes.**

Preston's functioning well. He's a cyber-doll. A robot. I invented him for food. But he's become free.

4 **Ask and answer questions.**

Did Preston grab Shaun? Who rescued Shaun? Where did they go?

55

SECTION THREE 02.20 TO 03.41

Before you watch

1 Look at page 60, Vocabulary.

📺 Watch section three.

After you watch

2 What happened? Use the pictures and describe the story to your partner.

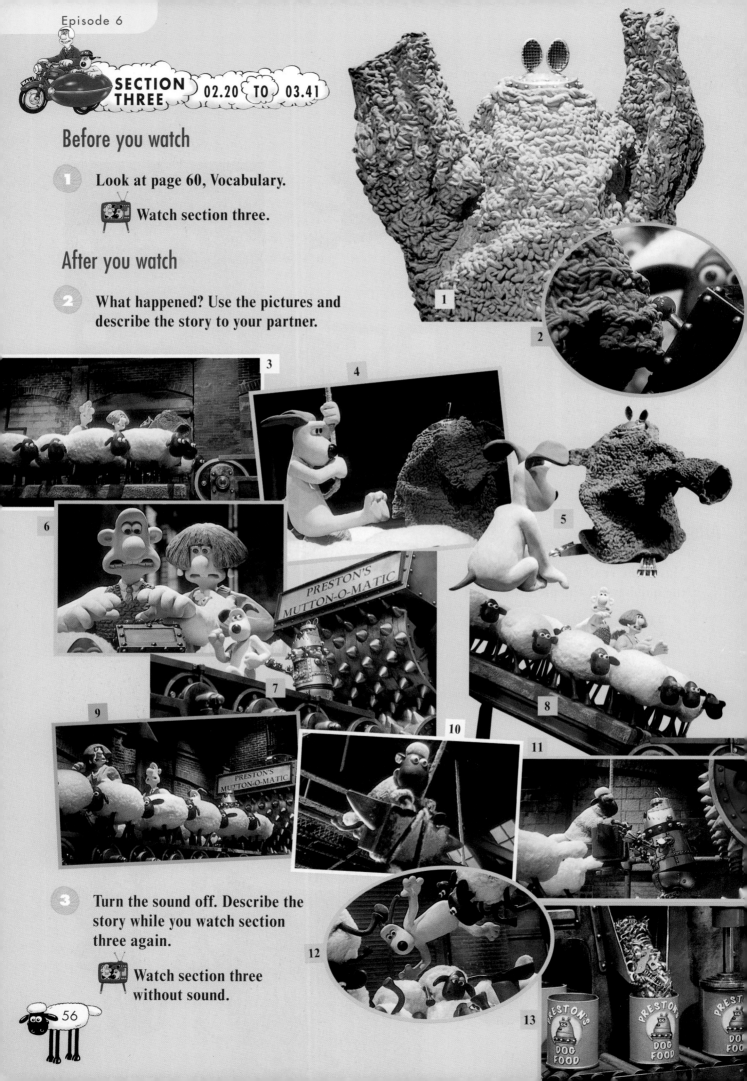

PRESTON'S MUTTON-O-MATIC

PRESTON'S MUTTON-O-MATIC

3 Turn the sound off. Describe the story while you watch section three again.

📺 Watch section three without sound.

PRESTON'S DOG FOOD

Start here

SECTION FOUR 03.41 TO 05.24

Before you watch

1 **What does the headline mean?**

Daily Beagle
GROMIT EXONERATED
HOOF-FRAMED GROMIT?

A   The police have given Gromit a medal.

B   The police have said that Gromit needn't go back to prison. They have forgiven him.

C   The police thought Gromit was guilty of sheep rustling, but now the police have said officially that he was never guilty.

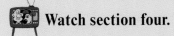 **Watch section four.**

While you watch

2 **Who says it? Write WAL for Wallace or WEN for Wendolene.**

1   Preston's back to normal.

2   Oh, don't mention it.

3   Thanks, boy.

4   You're very kind.

5   Why don't you come in?

6   We're just going to have some cheese.

7   I'm allergic to cheese.

8   I can't stand it.

9   Not even Wensleydale?

10   Goodbye ... chuck.

After you watch

3 **What did they say? Find their sentences.**

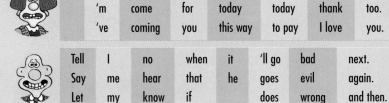

I	'll	came	here	to say	to say	thanks	to.
	'm	come	for	today	today	thank	too.
	've	coming	you	this way	to pay	I love	you.

Tell	I	no	when	it	'll go	bad	next.
Say	me	hear	that	he	goes	evil	again.
Let	my	know	if		does	wrong	and then.

4 **How is Wallace feeling? Why?**
e.g.

He looks (angry / sad / pleased / happy / unhappy / disappointed / depressed / annoyed).

He's (happy) because (he's just seen Wendolene).

5 **What happened to Preston? Ask and answer questions.**

See : Vocabulary, page 61, Preston's repairs

 Watch all of episode six again.

Watch the whole of 'A Close Shave' without stopping the video.

57

Exercises

1 Memory
Are these sentences true (✔) or false (✗)?

1 The second door was made of wood.

2 The plane spun round and Gromit shot out.

3 Shaun kicked Preston on to the conveyor belt.

4 Gromit knocked Preston into the mincing machine.

5 The machine crushed Preston.

6 Metal bits of Preston went into the cans.

7 Wendolene loves cheese.

8 Gromit repaired Preston.

Now correct the false sentences.

2 Test yourself
Choose the correct word in (brackets).

1 Pull (hardly / harder)!

2 He (don't / won't) like that!

3 He's (become / come) evil.

4 Here (comes / come) Shaun!

5 I've come here today (saying / to say) thank you.

6 I can't (understand / stand) it!

7 There's more cheese for (we / us).

8 And not a sheep (anywhere / nowhere).

Now check with the transcript on page 63.

3 What does she mean?

Wendolene says *Got to go home now*. She misses out words at the beginning. People often do this in conversation. She means:

I've got to go home now (or *We've got to go home now*).

What are the missing words?

1 Can't stay any longer. Sorry.

2 You going to come in?

3 Don't know!

4 Got to meet someone later. Must go.

5 See you tomorrow.

6 Hungry? I'll get you a biscuit.

4 What's it made of? Make true sentences.

Shaun's jumper	is	made of	metal.
Preston's jumper	are		steel.
The first door			copper. (Cu)
The second door			wood.
The wall			brick.
The Knit-O-Matic			wool.
Preston			dog hair.
The rollers			
The spikes			

5 Intonation

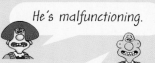

He's malfunctioning.

Mal-what?

Copy Wallace's intonation. Ask about these sentences in the same way.

He's a cyber-dog.   It's the Knit-O-Matic.

It's a machine for sheep mincing.

They're the sheep rustlers.

There was a wool shortage.

6 Sounds. Find the word in each line with a different vowel sound.
e.g.

Line 1: The different word is *robot*.

1	shot	wrong	robot	dog
2	come	home	rope	low
3	dive	dryer	wing	cyber
4	tube	duck	chuck	button
5	Shaun	normal	more	boy
6	clever	cheese	mention	propeller

Transfer

1 Survey. What did you think of 'A Close Shave'? Interview your partner.

You can use these expressions:

My favourite (picture) is ...
I liked (the picture on page 42) best.
I didn't like (this character) much.
I think (this one is the funniest).
I liked the music when (Wallace saluted Gromit) in episode five.

1 Who was your favourite character?
Wallace
Wendolene
Gromit
Preston
Shaun

2 Which was your favourite episode?
1 The uninvited guest
2 Love at first sight
3 The Knit-O-Matic
4 Crime and punishment
5 No escape
6 Gromit to the rescue

3 Look through this book. Which is your favourite picture?

4 Which is your favourite piece of music?

5 Which was the funniest scene? What happened in it?

6 Do you think Wallace and Wendolene are typically English?

2 Change partners. Talk about your first partner's answers.

Vocabulary

1 Machinery
Read this. Look at the bold words. Put them in the correct boxes on the picture.

This how the Mutton-O-Matic works. A **ramp** lifts the sheep up, then tilts. This sends the sheep onto the **conveyor belt**. The conveyor belt takes them to the mincing machine. The machine has two steel **rollers** with **spikes** on them. The rollers crush the sheep.

Gromit is kicking a ball.

2 Action verbs

Gromit's punching.

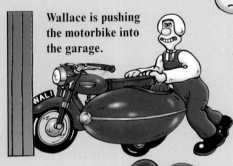

Wallace is pushing the motorbike into the garage.

Gromit's running.

Shaun is swinging on the rope. There's an anvil on the rope. He's holding on to it.

Wallace has knocked his head.

He's knocked the cup over.

The ramp is tilting.

3 Present participle / past tense / past participle

Present participle	punching	kicking	pushing	swinging	holding	tilting	knocking	running
Past tense	punched	kicked	pushed	swung	held	tilted	knocked	ran
Past participle	punched	kicked	pushed	swung	held	tilted	knocked	run

60

4 Wordplay

'Duck!' A *duck* is a water bird. The verb *to duck* means to lower your head so that something misses you. Wendolene tells Wallace *to duck* (Duck!). Wallace thinks she has seen *a duck* and asks 'Where?'.

'The Daily Beagle'
A *beagle* is a type of dog.

'Hoof-framed Gromit' People have *feet*. Dogs and cats have *paws*. Sheep, cows and horses have *hooves* (singular *hoof*).
When someone *frames* a person, they make them look guilty of a crime. 'Hoof-framed Gromit' is a play on words. It means *Who framed Gromit?* i.e. *Who made Gromit look guilty?*

6 Vocabulary notebook
Write translations. You can use your dictionary.

allergic arerugisei (0)	kicked keru
another	kind
anvil	knocked nokku suru / tataku
become	lift ageru koto
brick renga	— malfunctioning
can't stand	
chuck nageru/nagesuteru	mention te ni sureshite
clever	metal
conveyor belt	mincing hiku / komagire ni suru
cyber	mutton maton
depressed ochikondeiru	nasty iya / fukaina / hiretsuna
dive kyū kōka / tobikomi	nearly
duck moguru / mi o kagameru	normal
even (not even ...) / kaihi suru	propeller
ta ni ta ni de nai	punch genko / naguru suru
free	robot
get closer	run
get off	shot happō
go for mitomeru	tube chūbu / kuda
go wrong machigaeru	wings
(have) got to	wooden

5 Preston's repairs

Preston's holding a newspaper in his mouth. He's got wheels now, not legs. And he's got a bandage round his head.

Grammar

1 Sequence words

First ...	
Second ... (Third ...)	
Next ...	
Then ...	
Finally ...	

First he did this, then he did that. Next he did something else, and finally he stopped.

Note: we alternate between *then* and *next* for variety.

2 Invitations: *Why don't you ...?*

Why don't you (come in)?

Why don't you (sit down)?

Why don't we (go for a coffee)?

3 *looks*

That	looks	nasty!
This	sounds	nice!
It		
Those	look	interesting!
These	sound	dangerous!
They		

He	looks	happy.
She	sounds	sad.
You	look	angry.
They	sound	depressed.

He looks happy **because** Wendolene's just arrived.

4 Adverbs: *faster, harder*

Pull **harder!**

Run **faster!**

Walk **further!**

You're getting **closer**.

5 *made of*

It	is	made of	wool.
			steel.
They	are		metal.
			brick.

What's it made of? / What are they made of?

6 *Start doing*

I	started	learning	English	two years ago.
You		speaking	French	six months ago.
He		reading		last year.
She		writing		
We				
They				

The machine started shearing Preston.

The machine started knitting a jumper.

Expressions

Good shot!

Well done!

Here comes (Shaun).

Duck!

Back to normal.

Don't mention it.

Let me know ...

I can't stand (it).

Not even ...

There's one good thing ...

Go for (him).

SECTION ONE

Narrator Episode six, Gromit to the rescue.

Dive! Wings in. Wings in. Wings, Gromit. Too late. Fire!

Wallace Good shot, Gromit!

Narrator Preston's got the propeller. Shaun's got the rope. Pull, Shaun. Wallace is free. Pull harder! Now Preston's in the dryer. Shaun's got another idea. Close shave.

Wallace Well done, Gromit! He won't like that.

SECTION TWO

Wendolene He's malfunctioning.

Wallace Mal what?

Wendolene Malfunctioning. Preston is a cyber dog.

Wallace Cyber what?

Wendolene A robot. Daddy invented him for good. But he's become evil.

Wendolene He's going to grab Shaun!

Narrator No, he isn't.

Preston Grrr. Grrr. Grrr.

Wallace & Wendolene Aaah!

SECTION THREE

Wallace Huh? Ah. It's a sheep mincing machine. Now that's clever. Huh?

Narrator Gromit to the rescue!

Wallace Owww!

Narrator You're getting closer, Gromit. That looks nasty! Wrong button. That's faster. Run, Gromit!

Wendolene Do something, Wallace!

Wallace & Wendolene Whoah. Oooh!

Narrator Here comes Shaun!

Wendolene Duck!

Wallace Where?

Wallace & Wendolene Whoah. Oooh!

Shaun Baaa.

Wallace Oh, dear. We were nearly dog food, then.

SECTION FOUR

Wendolene I've come here today to say thank you. Preston's back to normal.

Wallace Oh, don't mention it. Thanks, boy. Let me know if he goes wrong again.

Wendolene You're very kind.

Wallace Why don't you come in? We're just going to have some cheese.

Wendolene Oh, no, not cheese. Sorry, I'm allergic to cheese. I can't stand it.

Wallace Not even Wensleydale?

Wendolene Got to go home now. Come on, Preston. Goodbye … chuck.

Wallace What's wrong with Wensleydale?

There's one good thing. There's more cheese for us. And not a sheep anywhere. Heh, heh. Get off my cheese. Get off … get off … Gromit! Gromit. Go for him. Go for him. Gromit! Oh! Get off my cheese. Oh. Oh. Oh, dear. Shoo off …

Shaun Baaa.

OXFORD
UNIVERSITY PRESS

Great Clarendon Street, Oxford OX2 6DP

Oxford University Press is a department of the University of Oxford.
It furthers the University's objective of excellence in research,
scholarship, and education by publishing worldwide in

Oxford New York

Auckland Bangkok Buenos Aires Cape Town Chennai
Dar es Salaam Delhi Hong Kong Istanbul Karachi Kolkata
Kuala Lumpur Madrid Melbourne Mexico City Mumbai
Nairobi São Paulo Shanghai Taipei Tokyo Toronto

Oxford and Oxford English are registered trade marks of
Oxford University Press in the UK and in certain other countries

ISBN 0 19 459243 X   Student's Book
ISBN 0 19 459244 8   Teacher's Book

ISBN 0 19 459240 5   VHS PAL Video Cassette
ISBN 0 19 459241 3   VHS SECAM Video Cassette
ISBN 0 19 459242 1   VHS NTSC Video Cassette

Printed in Hong Kong

Acknowledgments

Illustrations:
Mark Wagner
Bill Kerwin

Extra commissioned photography:
Mark Mason

*The publisher would like to thank the following for
their co-operation and assistance:*
Aardman Animations Ltd.
Alan Took at Pinewood Studios

Adaptor's acknowledgement:
The adaptors would like to thank the following people
at Oxford University Press for their commitment and enthusiasm:
Rob Maidment, who produced the ELT adaptation of *A Close Shave.*
Martyn Hobbs, who edited the ELT version.
Rob Hancock, who designed the Student's Book.
Tim Blakey, who edited the Student's Book.